Debt Elimination and Wealth
Creation for Beginners

Debt Elimination and Wealth Creation for Beginners

Baby Beginners *Presents*

Debt Elimination and Wealth Creation for Beginners

The Easy Way to Get Out of Debt and Build Wealth from Nothing

Michael Wells & Instafo

instafo

ISBN 978-1-072-01321-1

Printed in the United States of America

First Edition

Table of Contents

Chapter 1: The Unexpected Emergency Deficit

Chapter 2: The Real Financial Freedom

Chapter 3: The Debt Management 101

Chapter 4: The Financial Income Stream

Chapter 5: The Personal-Solid-Action

Chapter 6: The Debt-Free Living Destination

Chapter 1:

The Unexpected Emergency Deficit

Debt Cycle

Are you stuck in an endless, vicious cycle of **debt**? Do you dread the arrival of bills each month because you feel like you're digging yourself deeper into a hole and will never be able to climb out?

It's time to sort out your finances once and for all and eliminate those debts hanging around your neck. *We're going to help you.* But first, let's analyze the problem.

One of the biggest challenges with getting out of debt is the **interest** you have to pay on your unpaid balances. The longer you remain in debt, the more you will have to pay in the long run.

If you're like a majority of people, you get trapped in debt that you never really planned for. You spend freely and impulsively then find out that you are unable to pay.

Here are some examples:

- **A young man** obtained a student loan to finance his education, struggled to pass his courses, and then he couldn't find steady work to pay off the loan.

- **A businessman** took out a loan to expand his production cycle, but sales dropped and he was unable to pay off the loan.

- **An entrepreneur** got financial assistance from a colleague or bank to start a tech company and had a plan to pay the money back once the business turned a profit. But the business failed unexpectedly. Now he can't pay back the loan.

The <u>list</u> of such *unplanned debts* goes on and on.

Every debt has to be paid, but the payment terms differ from one situation to another. The sad thing is, some people owe so much to banks, colleagues, or the government that they wind up carrying their debts for their entire lives. *Imagine being stuck in debt forever!*

If debt is consuming your life, you don't have to be stuck like this forever. We will be covering a wide range of practical advice that should get you started with your quest to free yourself from debt.

Accidental Debtor

Studies have shown that many Americans stay in debt from college graduation all the way until death. The government has tried to help by implementing various tax breaks. But it's not always enough.

In our society, everybody has the opportunity to make money, yet more people are falling into the abyss of debt. So here's the <u>burning question</u>: *Why are people unable to pay back borrowed money?*

Human behaviors differ. There are people who lose sleep over debt while others borrow money without a care in the world and with absolutely no intention of paying it back.

Borrowing without a *concrete payback plan* is an easy way to fall into never-ending debt. But even if you borrow money and have a plan to pay it back, it doesn't always work out.

That's what we call **accidental debtors**. Accidental debtors are like the entrepreneur we mentioned earlier. They borrow to finance a particular project, which they hope would generate enough revenue to pay back the debt. But for unforeseen reasons, their plan fails.

We will now explore some of the common reasons why people get into debt and are unable to pay it back.

Business Venture

Every business owner dreams of success and being able to grow and expand their business. While plans for growth are typically captured in corporate business plans, expansions are often left out. Business expansion is one of the capital projects that requires a large amount of financial input. When it's time to expand, most business owners will apply for loans to help them finance the project.

The most common source of loans is **commercial banks**. A majority of these banks will not approve loans without **collateral** *equal to the amount of money being borrowed.* Essentially, this means if you want to borrow $7,000, you better *own something that's worth* $7,000, in case you default on the loan.

Even if you are lucky enough to have wealthy parents, friends, or siblings who agree to give you a loan without collateral, you will still need to pay them back unless they tell you otherwise. Failing to pay your debt is an easy way to ruin a good relationship. So, you may not be losing collateral but something bigger if you borrow from friends or family.

Here are a few things to consider to avoid plummeting into debt if you have a business or are planning to own one: *Do you know why banks require a <u>business plan</u> before giving out a loan?*

The <u>reason</u> is simple: *They want to make sure you have the business properly planned out so you can generate money to pay back the loan.* Banks understand that any venture that is not planned before execution is destined to fail.

Therefore, before you set up a business, do the following:

- Know the **target market** of your product or service, and focus your business there. For example, if you are interested in making clothes, look for the <u>age range</u> and <u>gender</u> whose market is always in demand. Also, think of the seasonality of the clothes you make. (Obviously, you won't sell many winter coats at the beginning of summer.)

- By **selling online**, you can expand your customer base beyond your immediate location to increase your revenue. In other words, if you live in a climate that's warm year-round, by selling online you can still target customers living in colder locations.

- **Liquidity** is the *ability to convert assets to cash for spending or investing.* If you have cash in the bank, it is your most liquid asset because you can instantly pull it out for its face value and use it for whatever you want to buy. Investment assets such as bonds typically take longer to convert to cash and may have restrictions about how you can use them. As soon as you start a new business, you should try to amass assets as much as possible. Assets can provide a cushion from debt. No matter how well you plan, plans don't always work out. When that happens, you can easily liquidate your assets and use the cash to finance your business rather than taking up bad loans with high interest rates that you may never be able to pay back.

Human Frailty

Psychologists say humans are constantly in search of happiness. It's hard to argue with that. *Don't you want to be happy?* We're basically wired to avoid pain, but we are never immune to it. When we face failing health, genetic disorders, cancer, and other degenerative diseases, we are forced to seek medical help.

Even if you are in good health, accidents happen to healthy people, and you could wind up in significant pain and bedridden for weeks or months. *Health care is expensive, no doubt.* If you do not have good health insurance or any health insurance, then you may resort to borrowing to pay for your health care.

So, during a period of illness or injury, you may be incapacitated not only physically but economically as well. You may be unable to work or do anything else that would help you make money to clear your debts.

While some of these human frailties are unavoidable, you should do all within your power to avoid whatever you can. Take absolute care of your health by sleeping at least five hours daily (or preferably more), including more fruits in your daily diet, and exercising at least three or four times a week for at least fifteen minutes. Meditation and yoga can work wonders and help your concentration.

See your doctor for regular medical checkups because preventing health problems is easier than curing them.

Natural Disasters

Various natural disasters have also sunk many people into unexpected debt. Earthquakes, tsunamis, flooding, wildfires, and mudslides seem to be on the rise around the world. Scientists blame some of these events on global warming.

The very fact that only a few people plan for natural disasters makes us prone to falling into debt when they occur.

A not uncommon example is a farmer who takes up a loan to be able to plant his crops. But then severe, unexpected flooding destroys everything, and his farm is uninsured. Suddenly, the farmer plunges into debt with no way to pay it back, and he has to borrow more money to take care of his family.

Natural disasters can leave the destruction of life and property at any time at anybody's path.

Plastic Plague

There is a plastic disease plaguing our society that is causing more debt than anything else. We're talking about "credit card." It is so easy for almost anyone to get a credit card these days. And that has become the *financial doom* of many Americans.

Credit card companies continuously lure customers with perks that make them continue to spend. Credit cards have many benefits, such as the convenience of getting whatever you need...even when you don't have enough money. However, the ease of spending has also led to the deepening of debt.

Credit cards have a psychological feel that encourages **impulse buying.** There's actually *less of a compulsion to spend* if you just have **physical money** in your pocket. But there's something about that little plastic card that *tempts* you to use it.

For example, when you pull out the money in your pocket and notice you are down to the last $10 bill, your subconscious automatically tells you to curb your spending habit. With a credit card, you just keep spending. This further validates the popular saying, *"Easy come, easy go."* In the end, when the credit card bill arrives, many Americans are scared to even look at it because they don't want to feel guilty about how much they spent.

To avoid credit card debt, it is important to have a good and regular source of income. Take time to read the terms and conditions before applying for a credit card. Some companies have lower interest rates and better grace periods. If you have to choose one of the other, it is better to get a credit card with a lower interest rate than one with a longer grace period. That's because longer grace periods make people complacent. They might think, *"Oh, I don't have to worry about paying this until next month."* Then they forget to pay it and fall into debt with an outrageous interest rate.

Now we are not saying to burn all your credit cards. To play a little bit of devil's advocate here, a credit card can be a great and easy way for any responsible beginner to build up their credit score. The best thing to do with a credit card is to keep tabs on every purchase. Most importantly, make plans to pay for *everything* as soon as possible.

Money Ignorance

One of the most paramount principles that you need to grasp is in *how to create wealth*.

Religious fanatics may be at peace with their debt by believing that some people are predestined to be poor no matter what and to simply accept their fate. Well, wealth can be hereditary because as humans, we learn by observing our environment.

Staying out of debt is the same way.

In his book *Rich Dad Poor Dad*, Robert Kiyosaki told us the way parents train their children and teach them about money is what makes them rich or poor. If you had parents who took being debt-free seriously, there is a huge chance you might unconsciously pick up that life principle and live by it as you get older.

Only those who are enlightened about how money works will understand they should only borrow when it is <u>absolutely necessary</u> and have a clear plan to pay it back.

Unfortunately, in school students are more likely to be taught how to *work for money* rather than *how money works*.

Indiscipline Unnecessity

If you read the book *The Richest Man in Babylon*, you will find out the reason why people are poor is that they don't have the discipline to control their cravings. In the book, Arkad taught his students the amount of money earned does not determine the affluence of such person. *Surprised?*

The reason is human desire is insatiable and nothing can be done about that. Many people think that buying a lot of things will make them happy. *But in reality*, what they buy is often what they don't really need. **Impulsive spending** and **lack of financial planning** are two behaviors that are destined to sink anyone into debt.

If you spend on everything that crosses your path, particularly when you have the insane urge to fit in with a wealthier social class, you will soon undoubtedly find out you are spending far more than you are earning.

Living life in the fast and flashy lane usually feels good at the moment. But the long-term effect is not always as rosy. You may need to find quick money, which is a fast way of inviting debt into your life.

Think about this example: A guy who wanted to live a glamorous lifestyle decided to invest in the stock market with hopes of getting rich quick. But he did not take the time to learn the skills needed for buying and selling stocks. *It didn't end well.* He lost all his money because he did not want to educate himself on how to invest wisely.

Gamblers can also quickly find themselves deep in debt. In fact, the shameful thing about gambling is it is a *game of luck.* Unfortunately, getting out of debt does not occur by chance. Addiction to gambling is a clear sign of impatience and lack of diligence to work and learn how to make money. It also shows a lack of self-discipline.

Starting a family without proper financial planning is another certain path to perpetual debt. If you want to avoid debt, you must understand this truth:

Wealth is just a progressive accumulation of riches and assets. It is not something that can happen overnight. That's why banks and other financial institutions talk about *self-management* first. Man cannot give what he does not have. If one cannot manage himself, he will find it difficult to manage anything else, including money.

Chapter 2:

The Real Financial Freedom

Creditor's Chained Collection

There is a parallel similarity between someone in debt and a slave. When you are in debt, you lose the freedom of living freely due to the fact your creditor is always somewhere around the corner to collect their dues. Your creditor—usually a bank—subconsciously controls your life. This control can even mentally affect where you can and can't go, or what you can and can't do.

The only way you can unshackle your chain to your creditor is to be debt-free.

Luckily, being debt-free has nothing to do with your financial status. It doesn't matter whether you have $10 in the bank or $10,000 in the bank. In either scenario, you may be deep in debt; just the same, in either case, you can be debt-free.

Why does it matter?

The main problem when you are in debt is that you'll find that you are unable to make the important financial decisions that would have a positive impact on your life.

Secure Financial Future

When you are free from debt, you will be in a better position to deal with any financial challenges that may come your way. When you are debt-free, you tend to worry less about your financial obligations, and this promotes peace of mind.

But if you owe money, you are basically working for the creditor or lender, even into old age of retirement. It's not always fun growing old. But it's a natural process that will happen to all of us if we're lucky enough to live a long time.

Let's look at <u>two categories</u> of people approaching retirement:

- The **first group** is those who are *anxious about their paycheck and retirement*. This group is apprehensive because, in retirement, you do not work as much and consequently will earn very little. Because these folks are concerned about it and are careful, the minimized income is usually a lesser worry.

- The **second group** just wants to *zip through life with abandon* and get to retirement age so they can enjoy their golden years. But life probably won't be so easy for them at retirement. Imagine someone in this group who has five or fewer years to work before retirement but still has a mortgage worth four times their annual salary. And perhaps they have a child in college. This person will likely be indebted until death.

In *Cashflow Quadrant*, another book written by Robert Kiyosaki, a rich dad told his sons to avoid debt at all costs. And if they must take on any debt, it should be small.

Here's why that is important: If you have a huge debt hanging around your neck, it's going to be awfully hard to think about saving money for the future. We all know the best form of financial security comes from savings.

People who are aware of the financial challenges of retirement usually start saving for it from their first paycheck. Retirement is supposed to be a time to rest, reminisce, and relax. Therefore, it is imperative that you prepare for this phase of life early so you can enjoy it.

One of the ways to prepare for this special time is by striving to be debt-free. Debt is like having a hole in your purse or pocket with all your hard earnings falling out. Being debt-free will help you to grow your retirement savings faster and plug that hole!

Easier Enjoyable Life

When you are in debt, you tend to work more and longer, yet sooner to your grave.

If you owe a ton of money, you're going to feel pressured to work as much as you can to pay it back. And this pressure increases your physical and mental stress. Excessive stress can negatively impact your health in several ways, including the risk of high blood pressure.

A person who is debt-free, on the other hand, will not have to worry so much about their paycheck or work so hard and, therefore, can choose to spend their money however they desire.

It goes without saying that medical experts have always recommended lowering stress in order to live a happier and healthier life.

Besides that, there are so many other benefits to be had once you pay off your debts, including:

- Spending money on the things that truly make you happy without the feeling of guilt.

- Improving your credit score, which is very important if you do need a loan or mortgage.

- Giving you the freedom of flexibility to easily change your life plans and goals.

- Going on a dream vacation and experiencing what you've been missing out on.

- Making your imagination run wild as you pursue creative pastimes.

- Having more time to spend with your friends and family.

To-Do: Obliged Obligation

There are a few ways you can test how debt impacts your life without actually sinking in debt.

Try this simple trick: Tell your friend something urgent has come up, and ask him if you can borrow some money (maybe $100, or any amount you can easily pay back). After you borrow the money, buy something nice (let's say a new smartphone that you don't need) and show it to your friend. *How do you think your friend will react?*

The kicker? While you're in debt to your friend, you'll find out how difficult it will be to say *"no"* to him.

You can even try borrowing from other close friends. You can take this experiment even further by deliberately failing to pay one of them back on the agreed date. Watch to see if their attitude toward you changes.

Dealing with Debt Collectors

Before we move on to the many practical applications to eliminating debt, this is something that is worthwhile for you to know: *how to deal with debt collectors.*

Being in debt makes you vulnerable to intimidation and harassment. If creditors clearly overstep their boundary while *"asking"* for the money back, you may be hesitant to complain about it because you feel guilty about your debt.

Creditors often hire **debt collectors** to help them recover debts. In Hollywood movies and television shows, they are usually portrayed as huge, muscular, ill-tempered guys in suits whose sole purpose is to "convince" you that you must pay back every penny right now!

If a creditor turns your debt over to a third-party collection agency, it can be more frustrating for you. These third-party collectors are companies that buy debt from the creditor at anywhere from <u>five</u> to <u>50 percent</u> of the debt. The third-party debt collector will try as much as possible to get you to pay, and in many cases will be very aggressive about it. Some can go as far as threatening to sue you, harm you physically, or even disrupt the peace of the neighborhood.

But even though someone is in debt, it does not mean they should be abused.

"The Fair Debt Collection Practices Act (FDCPA)" is a federal law that limits the behavior and actions of third-party debt collectors who are attempting to collect debts on behalf of another person or entity. The law restricts the means and methods by which collectors can contact debtors, as well as the time of day and number of times contact can be made."

Here are some of the <u>key provisions</u> of the FDCPA:

When Can Debt Collectors Contact Debtors?

Under the terms of the FDCPA, debt collectors cannot contact debtors at inconvenient times. That means they should not call before 8 a.m. or after 9 p.m. unless the debtor and the collector made an arrangement for a call to occur outside those hours. For example, if a debtor tells a collector that he wants to talk after work at 10 p.m., the collector can call. Without invitation or agreement, however, the debtor cannot legally call at that time.

Where Can Collectors Call Debtors?

Debt collectors can attempt to reach debtors at their homes or offices, but if a debtor tells a bill collector, either verbally or in writing, to stop calling his place of employment, the collector must not call that number again. Debtors can also stop collectors from calling their home phones, but they must put the request in writing.

If a bill collector does not have contact information for a debtor, he can call relatives, neighbors or associates of the debtor to try to find the debtor's phone number, but he cannot reveal any information about the debt, including the fact that he is calling from a debt collection agency. Additionally, collectors can only call third parties one time each.

What Can Debt Collectors Do?

Debt collectors can only tell a debtor about the debt and request payment. In some cases, collectors can work out a payment plan or settlement to help the debtor pay the bill. However, the FDCPA is designed to protect debtors from harassment by bill collectors. As a result, it is illegal for debt collectors to harass debtors, and in particular, they cannot threaten bodily harm or arrest. Additionally, debt collectors cannot threaten to sue debtors unless they truly intend to take the debtors to court.

<u>Chapter 3:</u>

The Debt Management 101

The Game Plan

The greater knowledge you have about money, the better personal financial manager you'll be. The reasons why people get into debt as already discussed make it evident that nobody is immune from falling into debt.

If it doesn't come from your own financial recklessness, it can be from natural disasters or a global economic meltdown, which happens almost every twenty to thirty years. It doesn't matter the source of your debt, the most important question now is: *What are the right steps to take for you to get rid of those debts?*

It's time to learn some new ways for paying off your debts and enjoying life again. There's no magic wand solution that will work for everyone. But we're going to give you a series of options and some valuable advice that can definitely help.

<u>Note</u>: Apart from financial education, all of the strategies and tips that follow from here on are aimed at helping you either *save more money* or *earn more money*. Every extra penny saved or earned should be channeled into paying off your debt.

Remember: *"A penny saved is a penny earned."*

– **Benjamin Franklin**

Minimalistic Makeover

Self-management is really the first and most important thing you need to know before anything else. *Why?* Because humans are the architects of their future. Unlike other animals, we make the bed that we lie on.

You have to realize that time spent cannot be regained. People are naturally inclined to relax and have fun, and in the process lose a lot of time they could have used for productive activities such as learning important life skills to help facilitate paying off debt.

A great aspect of self-management is adapting to the culture of **minimalism** of living below your means at very the bare minimum and getting rid of everything you don't need.

Is your home or apartment a mess? Several studies have shown that one of the most effective ways of improving your productivity is to **de-clutter**. At the very least, clutter can be a big source of distraction.

Are there any possessions you have that are adding to your financial burden? For example, do you really need a car while there are so many other cheaper transportation options out there? A car can easily bore a hole in your pocket with rising insurance costs.

If there is anything you own that you use only once a month or once every few months, chances are you can do without it.

To-Do: Patch Up Self-Inefficiency

We all have our time and money challenges. Self-management can help identify these loopholes and patch them up. To effectively deal with these issues, you need to be sincere with yourself.

The **first part of your task** will be to identify how much time you spend at work every day and how much time you spend on entertainment or just relaxing. Now, *give up some of your idle time for a productive activity* that will earn some money.

The **second part of this exercise** is to *find things in your home that you don't really need*, especially those things that may be getting in the way of your productivity. You may try selling those items, donating them to charity, or storing them out of the way until you really need them. Do an honest assessment of everything you own and think about how some of those things could yield money for you.

Take for instance, if you don't use your car that much, you could lend it to someone to use for a delivery service and collect some of the money they earn. On the contrary, if you do use the car every day to get to work but it's becoming a huge daily expense, consider selling it and taking public transportation.

If you are the type of person who travels out of town for extended periods of time, you could rent out your home and earn a nice fee.

You can save and earn money through minimalism, which is about living out the best of your life using the least resources.

Financial Intelligence

We all have a lot to learn when it comes to how our money works.

Through financial intelligence, you can discover how to make better financial decisions like identifying the difference between *needs* and *wants*. Financial intelligence also teaches you how to *prioritize* your needs.

This is something typically wealthy people always live by: Their money works for them. To elaborate this in the simplest way, they spend money to make money by channeling them into other investments.

This knowledge will help you to understand that debt is not bad in itself. What's bad are the factors surrounding the debt. Financial analysts say there are two types of debt: **good debt** and **bad debt.**

Good debt can actually be used wisely to expand a business. Analysts also consider a mortgage a good debt (as long as you don't buy more house than you need). Any investment in yourself for your future can also be a good debt, like your education.

Bad debt is anything that you don't need or losses its value over time, such as having multiple cars and the latest fancy gadgets.

To-Do: Become Financially Savvy

It's time to get financially literate. Many schools offer finance classes, and some of these schools even have online courses if you don't live nearby.

- One example is the University of Montana's (www.umt.edu/financial-education) online course called **"Transit,"** which is designed to help students take charge of their financial futures. The skill-based program walks students through the many ways they can manage their credit and debts. You can take advantage of this program too if you want to expand your knowledge of debt.

Now it doesn't have to be from an actual university. In the age of technology, there is no limitation to the acquisition of education and information out there. There are plenty of other online course websites: Udemy, Coursera, Lynda, Skillshare, etc.

So you can't make excuses. All you need is the internet. Hop on Google and do a search for *"financial literacy"* courses, and you should find plenty of options.

Economic Resourcefulness

Don't look at the journey toward being debt-free as a sprint, but a marathon. It takes discipline to keep working at it. The journey requires a great level of discipline, which could mean cutting down on your cravings for your savings. As a matter of fact, you can only be rich if you are able to reduce your excesses.

The book *The Millionaire Next Door* tells a story about a conference organized for millionaires. The organizers provided all sorts of flamboyant and expensive food. Surprisingly, the rich people attending the event did not touch the fancy food. They preferred simpler food, so they stayed hungry instead of eating from the elaborate spread.

Just like the wealthy people in the story, you need to realize that chasing after luxurious items and societal relevance will likely land you in serious debt if you are not careful. You see, the millionaires in the book knew that such foods were costly and probably tasted great. If they decided to eat the fabulous feast, they might have formed a habit and then wanted to eat like that all the time.

Let's say just for an example, the fancy meal cost $15, compared to a simpler meal for $10. The rich folks would prefer to eat the cheaper meal and then save the extra $5 for investing. Their line of thinking is they should try to spend *the least money* to get *the greatest comfort*.

The author of *The Compound Effect* explains this concept in a similar way. We'll stick with the example of the rich guy who preferred to spend $10 instead of $15 for food. Saving $5 may not seem much, but by changing your spending habits, it can add up to big savings over time.

Here's the simple math:

$5 x 365 days = $1,825

Imagine saving $1,825 every year and having that $5 compounded every month in some investment!

Now just because the rich man opted for less fancy food does not mean he couldn't eat healthy. *Far from it!* You can still make good food choices even when you spend less. Remember, eating too much junk food can lead to health problems, which will cost you more money.

Another great way to save is to do things yourself instead of hiring people. If you have a yard that needs mowing, you can buy your own lawnmower and take care if it yourself instead of paying someone else to do it. And then you can make extra money by mowing other people's lawns.

By solving your own problems, you reduce the risk of running into debt.

To-Do: Calculate, Budget and Pay

Building financial discipline is not easy, but having a **working budget** (preferably a monthly budget) can help you stay on track.

The first thing you need to do to plan an effective budget is to list all your income and expenditures. You can do this on your computer, or even on a piece of paper if you prefer the good old-fashioned way.

Make three columns: one for **income,** one **for expenditures/expenses,** and one for **debt.** Now answer this simple question: *Is your income enough take care of all your expenditures every month?*

– If "**yes,**" *how much is left?*

– If "**no**," *is there any expense you can remove from the list?*
How much would you save by eliminating some of those
expenses?

Now channel <u>whatever is left over</u> to taking care of the debt.
If you have more than one debt, consider these **two
methods** for paying them off:

Snowball Method: The snowball method is a debt
reduction strategy where you pay off your *smallest debt
first*, then when that first debt is paid off, you use the
money set aside for it to pay off the other debt. It
continues until all your debts are paid.

Interest Rate Method: The interest rate method,
sometimes called "the avalanche method," is a debt
reduction strategy where you pay off your debt that has
the *highest interest rate first*. Then when it's paid off, you
start paying off the debt with the next-highest interest
rate.

Both methods can be good. It may seem logical to pay off your debt with the highest interest rate first (the interest rate method) because in the end, you will pay less interest overall. But if you pay off your smallest debts first (the snowball method), it may give you the psychological satisfaction of paying off debts quicker. That satisfying feeling may help you stay on track with your finances.

Once you have sorted your income and expenditures, the next thing you should do that will help you stay disciplined is use a **budgeting tool**. There are lots of budgeting tools which you can use, and most of them come as apps for convenient smartphone use.

Once you download the budgeting app, you will be required to create an account. During the process, you will need to link your credit and debit cards. Some apps will alert you when you overshoot your budget for the month.

Some of the highly recommended budgeting apps include:

– **Mint** (www.mint.com)

– **PocketGuard** (www.pocketguard.com)

– **YNAB** (www.youneedabudget.com)

– **Wally** (www.wally.me)

– **Mvelopes** (www.mvelopes.com)

Chapter 4:

The Financial Income Stream

Working for Money

To start off, you'll need to have some consistent steady flow of income if you're going to have any fighting chance against debt.

On top of making sure that you have a job, do whatever side hustles you can to earn extra cash. No matter how much you've managed to save up, you're going to put that money into good use afterwards.

Billionaire Warren Buffet was able to save $10,000 after graduation because he had many part-time jobs as a college student. If you needed a loan to attend college, you can do the same thing Warren Buffet did with part-time jobs to pay it off.

If you think you don't have time for a part-time job, then it's time to re-assess how you use your time each day.

Try mapping out your day, and you might be surprised at how much time you spend doing unproductive things, particularly *financially unproductive* things. You can channel that wasted time into more work.

To-Do: Extra Work for Hire

If you're struggling with a lot of debt, you really should make better use of your spare time by picking up some extra work. Are there opportunities for overtime at your job? If you do shift work, maybe you can talk to your boss about working a double shift sometimes.

Another great way to generate some extra income is by working as a freelancer. Think about what skills you have that you can do from home on your computer. You can bid for freelance work on some of the big freelance sites, including:

– **Upwork** (www.upwork.com)
– **PeoplePerHour** (www.peopleperhour.com)
– **Freelancer** (www.freelancer.com)

You can register with these sites for free and create a freelancer profile. It is very important to create a complete profile to show prospective clients that you are a serious and diligent worker. Once your profile is set up, you can begin bidding for jobs based on your skills.

Investing for Money

To be debt-free and wealthy as well, you must consider **investing**.

Following the story of Arkad in *The Richest Man in Babylon*, one of the seven cures of a lean wallet is an investment. The book recommends entrusting your money to an expert. But maybe the expert is *you*. You can invest in anything, but the best thing you should invest in is what you know best. Put your knowledge to use. *What are your hobbies? What are your areas of expertise?* There's value in what you know.

Trying to invest in an unfamiliar field may warrant hiring an expert. There's a balance you have to keep in mind, though. Hiring an expert should be beneficial to your results, but the money you pay the expert is money you could have used to pay off your debt faster. When you are trying to get out of debt, it is important that you cut down your expenditures as much as possible. Remember that when you consider hiring an expert.

To get started, visit your nearest brokerage. Most banks already have a brokerage division; there's Merrill Edge offered by Bank of America and TD Ameritrade by TD Bank.

If you feel comfortable enough, you can do it all on your own online without a broker.

We recommend these online brokerages that are best suited for beginners because they're simple and, best of all, free to use without the typical fees.

– **Robinhood** (www.robinhood.com)
– **M1 Finance** (www.m1finance.com)

It is also pertinent to know that most investments demand patience. We're talking long term here. The reward for investment is usually larger but may take many years before you can start reaping the full benefit. And sometimes investments rise and fall rapidly, like a roller coaster.

Example:

Let's say you're a soda drinker, and your beverage of choice is Pepsi, so you want to buy stock in the company as an investment. If you buy 200 shares of Pepsi in January for $5 each, it will cost $1,000. Then, suddenly in March, there's a big drop in Pepsi stock, and now the shares only cost $3, for a total value of $600. *Oh no, you've lost $400!* Now you have a choice: **panic** or **patience**. If you have faith in the company, you'll opt for patience by staying calm and riding out the losses. You may even buy up more shares of Pepsi stock at the cheaper cost because eventually, the stock will rise again.

Of course, this is merely a *hypothetical example.* There are always other factors involved, including tax implications. If you decided to sell your stock after the price dropped, there would likely be a tax deduction due to losses incurred. It would be a good time to consult a tax expert before you decide what to do.

If you have no intention of investing in stocks, there are various safer options out there that we will discuss next.

Bonding for Money

Have you considered investing in Uncle Sam? There are several categories of bond investments with the United States Treasury. The one with the *lowest risk* is the **Treasury Inflation Protection Securities (TIPS).**

Investing is like trying to swim in murky waters because of the risk. So if you are cautious about losing your money, TIPS is probably the best option for you. The bond grows at a fixed interest and also grows depending on the inflation level.

Here is how it works:

The U.S. government issues special bonds, usually used to help the government raise money for certain initiatives to be paid back at a set maturity date with interest.

For example, if you bought a bond worth $500 for $300, which has a maturity date of **25 years**, it means at the expiration of that date you can redeem your bond for a minimum of $500. It is a guaranteed investment, but just like many *low-risk* investments, the reward is also *low*.

Another benefit of a U.S. bond is the interest is not taxed. If you are interested in this type of bond, you can invest at **Treasury Direct** (www.treasurydirect.gov/indiv/myaccount/myaccount_treas urydirect.htm) or through your broker.

Banking for Money

A high-yield account provides a higher interest rate than your traditional savings account will ever offer you. The annual percentage these accounts offer ranges from <u>one</u> to <u>two</u> percent or higher.

Several online and brick-and-mortar banks offer **high-yield savings accounts**. Opening a high-yield saving account is basically the same process as opening a normal savings account except the terms will differ.

It's always good to shop around and see what's out there. Here are a few banks with high-yield savings accounts to consider:

- **<u>Ally Bank</u>**: (<u>www.ally.com</u>) This one may be the most well-rounded online bank with just about every service that traditional banks have, from credit cards to checking, savings, and CD accounts. Ally offers a 2.20 percent interest rate on their savings account. And their checking account even gives you a 0.60 percent interest rate, more than the CD and savings account you probably have now.

- **CIT Bank:** (www.cit.com/cit-bank) This is another online bank that offers as much as a 2.45 percent interest rate on savings accounts.

- **Purepoint:** (www.purepoint.com) This bank offers attractive rates for savings accounts and CDs.

- **Marcus by Goldman Sachs:** (www.marcus.com/us/en) Goldman Sachs is a well-established brand that millions of people trust.

- **Barclays Bank:** (www.banking.barclaysus.com/index.html) In addition to a savings account with a great rate, this bank also has a credit card with a good rewards program.

It's worth taking the time to compare savings account interest rates at these banks and others. If you are currently earning a minuscule interest rate at your local bank, then *what the heck are you waiting for?!* It's shameful not to switch over at least some funds to these higher-earning online banks. On average, they're about nineteen times more than what you will get at any traditional bank.

Banks that only operate online can typically offer better rates because they have fewer expenses (for example, not having to own real estate or pay as many workers). The money you earn on a savings account won't make you rich, but it can go a long way in generating more cash to help pay off your debts.

If you do choose an online bank, be aware that there are no physical locations. So if you prefer the old-fashioned feel of walking into a branch and talking to a bank employee face-to-face, that won't be possible. And banks that don't have physical branch locations also don't have their own ATMs.

But some online banks will reimburse a portion of your ATM fees each month if you use other banks' ATMs.

So just keep these things in mind if you decide to abandon your brick-and-mortar bank entirely. Banks with branch locations are indeed convenient for depositing, withdrawing, and transferring money.

The good news is online banks are just as safe as physical banks. Both are insured by FDIC, so if the bank goes belly-up, your money is protected up to a certain point.

Lending for Money

Do you have a little extra cash in your account and want to help out others in need? You could loan them the money with a small interest rate, perhaps three to eight percent. It doesn't have to be a huge loan.

Maybe you have a buddy who's coming up a little short on money for next month's rent or car payment. It's an opportunity for you to help as well as generate a small amount of extra cash when they pay you back.

- If you want a low-risk lending option, take a peek at **Worthy Bonds** (www.worthybonds.com). It offers a five percent return, and your input is liquid. So you can take out your cash at any time.

- **Lending Club** (www.lendingclub.com) is a good one to look at too. Make sure you adjust the amount of risk you're willing to take based on borrowers' credit score. The lower their credit score is, the higher the risk of you're not going to be paid back, but you'll receive a higher potential ROI from the higher interest rate.

Something to keep in mind is that some of the borrowers couldn't get a loan the conventional way through a bank, so that's why they're turning to peer-to-peer lending. To weed out the bad apples, be selective with whom you to lend to.

Owning Assets for Money

Wouldn't it be great to earn money while not actively working? Imagine just sitting back and watching some extra cash show up in your bank account. That's known as "passive cash flow," and it's something we would all love to have. Basically, you are being paid over and over again for work that you do only once. Now you're probably thinking: *"Great! Where do I sign up?"*

Obtaining and owning assets is one of the most valuable things you can do with your money (besides paying off your debt, of course). When you own an asset that generates passive income, it makes it easier for you to pay your debts.

Real estate is the pinnacle of what people think by default when it comes to passively getting wealthy. Maybe you've seen some of those real estate shows on TV where ordinary people purchase as many properties as they can then rent them out for monthly passive income. Or they fix-up the houses to increase their market value then sell them for huge profits. That's called "flipping."

Of course, there's a lot of behind-the-scenes work involved in doing all that, not to mention the headaches, time, and risks involved. (Ever seen the psychological-horror movie *Pacific Heights* with Michael Keaton? You'll witness every landlord's worst nightmare and laws that are not always in their favor.)

Most of all, the biggest hurdle that prevents people from getting into real estate is the initial investment capital. You need a lot of money, plain and simple. And there's also a fear factor. The thought of buying and selling real estate can be intimidating.

Well, guess what? Times have changed thanks to modern technology. You don't have to be a licensed realtor—or a real estate genius—to get into the game. The fact is, investing in real estate is now easy for everyday people like you. Check out these real estate investment platforms:

- **Fundrise:** (www.fundrise.com) Fundrise is a crowdfunded real estate investment opportunity that lets you begin investing with as little as $500, and you never have to set foot on any properties but can view them from your computer.

- **Rich Uncles:** (www.richuncles.com) If you aren't ready to fork over $500, then Rich Uncles may be for you. On this platform, all you need is $5 to start investing! Look for the "BRIX REIT" investment option.

- **Realty Mogul:** (www.realtymogul.com) Reality Mogul is another one to consider if you have $1,000 available to invest.

The money you invest for these real estate platforms helps fund their real estate projects to increase value appreciation. On top of that, you also earn dividend payment, which you can withdraw that dividend or reinvest it for an even higher payout in the end.

Sounds attractive, right? So what's the catch?

Yes, every investment has risks. But these real estate investments are viable options and definitely worth considering. Just keep these things in mind:

- These should be long-term investments. So if you want to use your entire real estate investment fund to pay off something in a hurry, you won't have immediate access to it. It takes time to get your return. Remember when we discussed **liquidity** earlier? (*Go back and refer to that again if you need to.*) Real estate has the <u>least liquidity</u> of any kind of investment.

- While this is a very hands-off way to get involved in real estate, your **return on investment (ROI)** will always *be less* than if you were to directly invest that money in a property yourself. For example, if you happen to have $5,000 saved up to invest, you're better off owning a real physical property on your own than investing that $5,000 in virtual real estate crowdfunding with much *smaller ROI*. But the tradeoff is, with a virtual investment you don't have to do any of the extra work involved in managing and fixing up the property.

• Finally, be aware that these concepts are *still relatively new*, so there is no way to predict the future or if you might lose the money you invested if something happens to whatever platform you're using, especially during a downturn in the market like that of the 2008 financial crisis. We're not trying to scare you. It's just important to understand the risks of any investment.

But really, aside from the risks, these newer, easier methods for investing in real estate sound pretty cool, don't they?

There is a reason why real estate remains as the most popular form of assets.

"Buy land, they're not making it anymore."
– Mark Twain

To-Do: Profit from Possessions

While we're still on the topic of real estate, sit down and think about whatever possessions you own and the options you have for using some of your assets to earn extra easy cash. Even if you generate a small amount each time, it adds up over the long haul.

If you have a spare room in your house or apartment, or if you have something like a car that you hardly ever use, you can rent it out for passive profit to use for reducing your active debt.

To-Do: Determine Your Route

Draw up your economic plan for the next <u>five years</u>. The economic plan should answer the following questions:

1. How much do I earn in a year?

2. How much does it take to satisfy my basic needs like water, food, transportation, health care, etc.?

3. Do I need more than what I have in savings to satisfy my needs?

4. If "*yes*," what can I do to get more savings from my earnings?

5. Where do I see myself in the next five years?

6. What steps should I take to get there?

7. What and how best do I invest in order to get to where I want to be in the next five years?

8. How best do I cushion myself against financial accidents or market crashes?

9. Who is my financial adviser, and is this person knowledgeable in the areas I am interested?

If you discover after answering the <u>first four questions</u> that your earnings are not taking care of your basic needs (even when you are trying to spend very little), it means you are *not earning enough*.

Your **primary goal** should be to *increase your earnings* first, then worry about savings second. Choose one or two options from the prior sections to help you make additional cash.

Chapter 5:

The Personal-Solid-Action

The Con in Consolidation

You know your debt is really out of hand when **the interest** that piles up over time *becomes even bigger than* **the original amount** you owed in the first place.

For example, if you borrowed $2,000 at an interest rate of 6 percent in 2015, and did not pay till 2019, the amount payable will be $2,600 using the simple interest rate. If you drag out the payments even longer, what you owe in interest will eventually exceed the original $2,000.

This calls for a *serious work* toward paying off debt on time because the longer you wait, the bigger your debt gets.

What about "**debt consolidation**"? It's applicable if you have different types of debts such as credit card, student loan, and car payment and want to make them more manageable by combining them all into one huge debt. Yet, if you have bad spending and saving habits, debt consolidation is not going to make any difference whatsoever.

According to popular finance expert Dave Ramsey who prominently advocates debt-free living and helps many people get out of debt, debt consolidation is overrated as another form of financial product that you're buying into that looks great on the surface but keeps you in debt longer and should be avoided. It's more for damage control and giving you breathing space with extended periods of time to pay off your one huge debt in smaller amounts; however, in the long run you're actually paying far more.

Lenders are perfectly happy to sit back and watch you stretch out your payments (as long as you are least making the minimum payment each month). *Why?* Because you are helping the bank make more money. The longer you drag out your loan payments, the more money the bank earns because of the *interest* you will have to pay.

That is why you don't want to be in debt longer than you have to. The better thing to do is to take the *"con"* out *"con-solid-ation"* and opt for *"personal-solid-action."*

Nevertheless, if you still insist on consolidating, talk with your bank about taking out a debt consolidation loan. *If you get approved,* that's great! *If not,* there are plenty of other third-party lenders out there that are not banks and are less stringent about credit score but with higher interest.

The Credit Score Factor

Debt can ruin your reputation. Defaulting on your payments can also hurt your relationship with your friends.

However, the long-lasting negative impact of debt is usually on **your credit score.**

A bad credit score will make it difficult for you to get a loan in the future. One day that may hurt your chances of buying a house or a car.

If you know you will be needing credit in the near future, it is important to pay attention to your credit score. Keep in mind, your credit score will not improve overnight. But there are some behavioral changes that you can help you get there over time. If you are in doubt about your credit score, it is important to check it frequently.

Look for the "**Free Credit Report**" link at www.bankrate.com.

- **Don't worry about trying to get old debts removed from your credit report.** If you paid off those old debts on time, then that's actually good for your credit history and score. The longer you leave "good" old debts on your credit record, the better it is for your credit score. It shows that you are financially responsible.

- **Pay off debts as quickly as possible.** Paying quickly is very important to your credit score. One way to make sure you pay back debt on time is to make plans to pay back before borrowing. In other words, don't even take out the loan until you have a strategy in place for paying it back.

- **Take out loans only when it is absolutely necessary.** Some people are in the habit of taking out loans to buy just about anything. A smarter thing to do is to only take credit when it is truly needed. Sometimes, the best way to keep a good credit score is not to engage in behaviors that would put it at risk in the first place.

A Simple Three-Step Process

If you are faced with a daunting project, it can be so tempting to put it off for as long as possible. Don't let this happen to you if the daunting project is to pay off your debt.

Yes, we know it's not always fun to tackle your financial challenges head-on. But there are <u>three steps</u> you can take to make your debt payment easier:

<u>STEP 1</u>: Break down the debt into smaller amounts. Charging <u>$6,000</u> on your credit card will only take seconds, but paying back the same amount may not be so easy. You can break down the payment to something like <u>$150 monthly</u>, or <u>$50 weekly</u>, or <u>$10 daily</u>. A financial calculator (<u>www.nomoredebts.org/learning_credit/calc.html</u>) will help you to calculate how to expedite your debt payment.

STEP 2: **Create a spending plan.** Carve out a budget or spending plan that takes into account your small payments. Once you have created a budget, avoid impulse spending and stick with your budget.

STEP 3: **Expedite your payments by seeking other sources of income.** Because your spending is guided by a budget, you'll need to earn extra money in order to be able to make higher debt payments.

Remember that *"slow and steady"* wins the race. Unless you win the lottery or inherit a fortune from a rich relative, you won't be able to clear your debts in one swoop.

But you can do it if you commit to taking the time needed to break down what you owe into increments that you can pay over time, and you make a disciplined commitment to follow the payment schedule.

To-Do: Apply Snowball or Interest Rate Methods

Let's review the **snowball** and **interest rate methods** of paying off debt and put them into action with these exercises. If you want to pay off your debt using the snowball method, here's how to go about it:

- Line up your credits in the increasing order (*smallest balance* first, followed by the next smallest, etc.).

- Divide your paycheck into <u>three parts</u>: One-third will be used to pay off debt. To make the math easy, we'll say your pay is <u>$100</u>. In that case, you would use <u>$33</u> to pay off debt.

- Pay <u>$33</u> from each check toward paying off your *smallest debt*. Continue like this until it is paid in full.

- When the smallest credit has been paid off, roll over the $33 that should have been used for it into the next smallest credit.

- Do likewise for others until all the debts are settled.

The snowball method is best for you if paying off one debt in full will *excite you and motivate you to pay off more*.

But if you prefer the interest rate (or avalanche) method, here's what you do:

- Line up the credits in the descending order of their interest rate. Start with the credit that has the *highest interest rate*, then list the second highest, etc.

- Set aside the money for debt settlement. We'll keep using the $100 paycheck example. Use $33 from each paycheck toward the debt with the highest interest rate. Once that one is paid off, move to the second highest interest rate.

- Continue in that manner until everything is paid off.

The interest rate method is best for you if you want *to pay the least total amount over time.*

A Financial Advisor's Five-Step Process

Let's now turn to *New York Times* bestselling author and financial advisor Ramit Sethi, who wrote the book *I Will Teach You To Be Rich.* (Who wouldn't want to learn that?) He has a five-step process for getting out of debt.

If you're one of the 80 percent of all Americans in debt (and you must be if you're here to begin with), then you need to pay attention to the following steps.

STEP 1: Admit you are in debt and organize *all you owe.* Yes, admitting your debt is an important first step. *Why?* Because some people feel so guilty about their debt, especially excessive credit card spending, that they don't even want to look at their bills to see how much they spent. Living in denial of debt may be soothing, at least temporarily. But let's be frank. Denying your debt isn't going to make it go away.

If you use your credit cards with abandon and just send in the minimum payments each month, you will never—that's right, NEVER—get out of debt. Coming to terms with the truth can be the turning point you need to get out of the cycle of debt. If you are not sure how much you owe, access your account online or call your credit card company. The phone number is right there on the back of the card. You may discover that figuring out exactly how much you owe is the hardest part of getting off debt. But once you do it, then you can move forward with doing something about it.

If you use more than one credit card, you can design a table like the one shown to track your debt:

Name of Credit Card	Total Debt	APR	Minimum Payment per Month

STEP 2: Order your debts in how they will be paid off. Different credit card companies charge varying interest rates. If you have other debts besides credit cards, those will have different rates too. Pay off the debt that has the highest interest rate first if you prefer the "**interest rate method**" we explained earlier. For example, if **Credit Card A** has a 12 percent interest rate, while

Credit Card B has a six percent interest rate, you will save more by paying off **Credit Card A** first.

For student loans, you can gain more by paying more every month. For example, if you took a student loan of $10,000 with a 10-year repayment period at an interest rate of 6.8 percent, it means you would be required to pay about $115 every month. The total interest you would pay if you stick to this minimum amount would be $3,810. However, if you decide to pay $415 every month, you would end up paying only $782 interest. Paying only the minimum amount of any debt *isn't* going to get you out of debt.

STEP 3: Control your cravings. If you always have credit cards in your wallet, then you're always going to be tempted to use them. So take them out and leave them at home. If you're struggling to get out of debt, digging yourself deeper into debt by using your credit cards is totally counterproductive.

STEP 4: Discuss a lower interest rate with your credit card company. Just because the interest rate is listed on your bill every month, that doesn't mean it's set in stone. Call your credit card company and negotiate a lower interest rate on your card. All you have to do is ask. With a lower rate, you will automatically save money every month.

STEP 5: Start paying off your debt: The money saved from **STEP 4** should be used to pay off debt just like the money saved from self-management and conscious spending plan.

Alternatively, you can opt for ways to earn extra income to pay off debt. You really need to consider all the options we mentioned before and choose those that best suit you.

<u>Chapter 6:</u>

The Debt-Free Living Destination

Getting *into debt* is easy, but getting *out of debt* is a different story.

Debt itself is neither good nor bad. It all depends on your financial acumen. And now that you've made it almost to the end, you should be ready to put a plan into action that will get you on the road to clearing your debt.

To be debt-free, invest in financial education because it goes a long way in improving how you handle your money. If you must get a loan, make sure you have a solid plan for how you will pay it back. This isn't just for bank loans or credit card debts. You also must plan for paying back the money you've borrowed from friends and family unless it was truly given as a gift.

Remember that reducing or eliminating your debt requires financial discipline, prudence, and some level of frugality. It is good to save and invest your money. But investing requires caution due to risk. So invest in areas you know, or get a good financial advisor.

The journey toward becoming debt-free is not easy, but you can do it! We've stressed the importance and benefits of being debt-free from the very beginning. Keep this as a resource so you can refer back to it as you plan your escape from debt.

You can live a happier and healthier life once you make a conscious effort to pay off your debt. It all starts with a firm commitment. Once you have made up your mind, stand up, roll up your sleeves and get to work.

Soon you'll realize that the endless cycle of debt isn't endless after all!